CONTENTS

KU-507-005

CHAPTER 1

Nigeria –
An Overview

Nigeria is the most populous country in Africa and also one of the most powerful countries on the continent. It is sometimes called the 'Giant of Africa'. When many people think of Nigeria they often imagine a country that is chaotic, dirty and noisy, with a reputation for crime and corruption. Although these are very real problems that affect large parts of the country, there is much more to Nigeria. It boasts, for example, one of the richest and most complex cultures in Africa, thanks to the extraordinary diversity of its population, which consists of over two hundred and fifty ethnic groups and speakers of more than four hundred languages.

Nigeria's three main religions, Christianity, Islam and traditional beliefs, add to this cultural diversity. Islam, in particular, has had a major impact in northern Nigeria, where it is an important influence on everyday life. For example, Sharia law (Islamic law) has been adopted in several of the country's northern states. Despite their differences, there are aspects of culture that many Nigerians share – especially the value they place on family life and extended family networks and the importance they give to ceremonies and social events.

 Did you know?

The Nigerian flag uses green to symbolize the land and fertility, and white to symbolize peace and unity.

A WASTED OPPORTUNITY?

The discovery of oil in the country in the 1950s brought great hope to the people of Nigeria. Other countries around the world had seen rapid improvements in their standard of living following the discovery of oil, the most valued natural resource on the planet. Nigerians felt further optimism when their country gained its independence from the United Kingdom (UK) in 1960, ending almost one hundred years of colonial rule. Unfortunately, their hopes were short-lived. Successive governments (most of them military-controlled) mismanaged the oil revenues. Far from benefiting from the newfound oil wealth, most Nigerians have seen drops in both their standards of living and their incomes.

The misuse of oil revenues and the failed hopes of millions of Nigerians have been a source of great tension and unrest in the country. Almost since independence, Nigeria has been disturbed by civil unrest, as different groups have competed for power and access to land and resources. Because these competing groups have usually had strong ethnic and religious identities, the unrest and tensions have gone far beyond politics and have become part of everyday life.

▶ Young girls in traditional Nigerian dress. Although Nigeria has seen many changes in the last few decades, certain customs and traditions, such as the way the birth of a child is celebrated and the type of food people eat, remain strong.

World in Focus
Nigeria

WAYLAND

ALI BROWNLIE BOJANG AND ROB BOWDEN

First published in 2006 by Hodder Wayland,
an imprint of Hodder Children's Books

© Hodder Wayland 2006

This paperback edition published in 2009 by Wayland,
an imprint of Hachette Children's Books, 338 Euston Road, London NW1 3BH.
www.hachettelivre.co.uk

Commissioning editor: Victoria Brooker
Editor: Kelly Davis
Inside design: Chris Halls, www.mindseyedesign.co.uk
Cover design: Hodder Wayland

Series concept and project management by EASI-Educational Resourcing
(info@easi-er.co.uk)
Statistical research: Anna Bowden

Maps and graphs: Martin Darlison, Encompass Graphics

British Library Cataloguing in Publication Data
Bojang, Ali Brownlie
   Nigeria. - (World in focus)
   1. Nigeria - Juvenile literature
   I. Title
   966.9'054

ISBN: 978 0 7502 4695 8

Printed and bound in China

Cover top: Farmer preparing fields at the beginning of the rainy season near Maiduguri, Borno State.
Cover bottom: Hausa/Fulani girls near Dutse, Jigawa State.
Title page: Women selling potatoes at a local market, near Vom on the Jos Plateau.

Picture acknowledgements
The author and publisher would like to thank the following for allowing their pictures to
be reproduced in this publication:
Corbis 10 and 25 (Reuters/George Esiri), 12 and 13 (Bettmann), 34 (Reuters/Mike Segar),
35 (Reuters/Finbarr O'Reilly), 36 (Reuters/Jason Reed); EASI-Images/Roy Maconachie cover
top and bottom, title page, 8, 14, 20, 28, 33, 39, 43, 46, 48, 55, 57 and 59; EASI-Images/Lorena Ros
5, 6, 9, 11, 15, 16, 17, 19, 21, 22, 23, 24, 26, 27, 29, 30, 31, 32, 37, 38, 40, 41, 42, 44, 45, 47, 49(t),
49(b), 50, 51, 52, 53, 54, 56 and 58.

The website addresses (URLs) included in this book were valid at the time of
going to press. However, because of the nature of the Internet, it is possible that
some addresses may have changed, or sites may have changed or closed down
since publication. While the author and Publishers regret any inconvenience this
may cause the readers, no responsibility for any such changes can be accepted
by either the author or the Publisher.

The directional arrow portrayed on the map on page 7 provides only an approximation of north. The data
used to produce the graphics and data panels in this title were the latest available at the time of production.

A NEW BEGINNING

In 1999, after almost three decades of military rule, Nigeria returned to civilian, democratic government. Despite the many hardships still faced by Nigerians, people were optimistic that this was the beginning of a new era of democracy and freedom. Nigeria still has a good chance of becoming a prosperous country in which the majority of Nigerians benefit from their nation's riches. Its vast oil reserves give it global strategic importance; it is rich in natural resources, many of which are currently under-exploited or not exploited at all; and it has a dynamic and relatively well-educated population.

There are new opportunities too, such as a share in the global tourist industry – the world's fastest-growing industry. Nigeria possesses

tropical forests, deserts and beautiful beaches. Its long history, spanning several different civilizations, has also left it with a legacy of exceptionally beautiful arts and crafts and ancient walled cities and villages, many of which have barely changed in thousands of years. These could help to make Nigeria an attractive tourist destination. The first challenge for Nigeria, however, is to overcome the damage inflicted on the country in the past by corrupt military regimes. With the return of democratic government, foreign investors are slowly coming back and between 2003 and 2007 the value of the economy doubled. But, at the start of the twenty-first century, Nigeria still has far to go before meeting the unrealized ambitions of its ever-optimistic people.

▼ Nigeria has the second-largest economy in Africa, with major businesses (often connected to oil) and hundreds of smaller local businesses providing for local needs.

Physical geography data

- Land area: 910,768 square kilometres/351,648 square miles
- Water area: 13,000 sq km/5,019 sq miles
- Total area: 923,768 sq km/ 356,667 sq miles
- World rank by area: 32
- Land boundaries: 4,047 km/2,513 miles
- Border countries: Benin, Cameroon, Chad, Niger
- Coastline: 853 km/530 miles
- Highest point: Chappal Waddi (2,419 metres/7,936 feet)
- Lowest point: Atlantic Ocean (0 m/0 ft)

Source: CIA World Factbook

 Did you know?

In 2005, 14.6 per cent of all Africans (about one in seven) was a Nigerian.

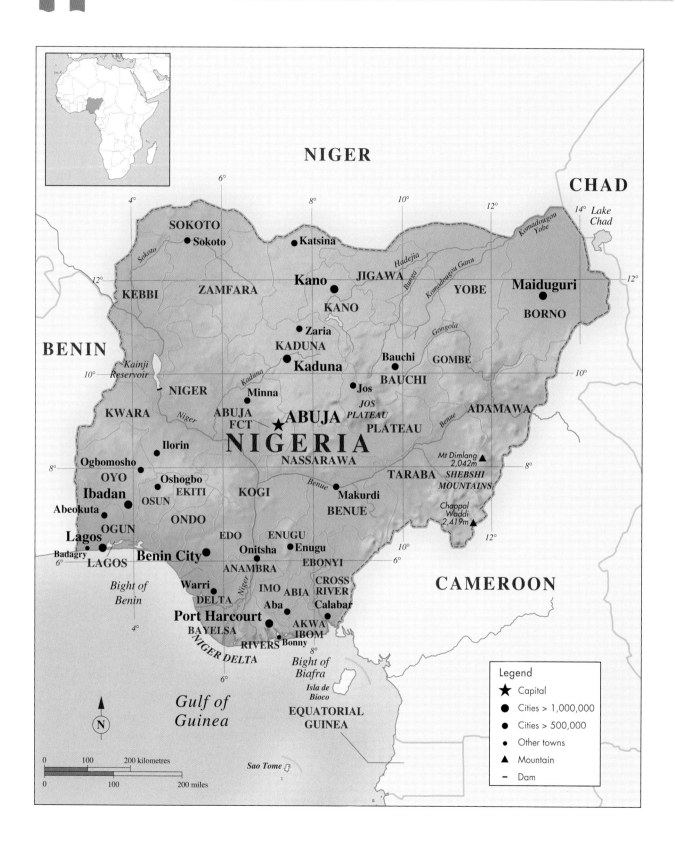

NIGER

CHAD

BENIN

CAMEROON

EQUATORIAL
GUINEA

*Gulf of
Guinea*

*Bight of
Benin*

*Bight of
Biafra*

*Isla de
Bioco*

Sao Tome

SOKOTO
● Sokoto

● Katsina

Kano
●
KANO

● Zaria

KADUNA
● **Kaduna**

● Minna

ABUJA
FCT
★ **ABUJA**

NIGERIA

NASSARAWA

KEBBI

ZAMFARA

JIGAWA

YOBE

Maiduguri
BORNO

● Bauchi
BAUCHI

GOMBE

● Jos
JOS
PLATEAU
PLATEAU

ADAMAWA

TARABA

SHEBSHI
MOUNTAINS

Mt Dimlang
2,042m ▲

Chappal
Waddi
2,419m ▲

NIGER

KWARA

Ilorin ●

Ogbomosho ●
OYO
Oshogbo ●
EKITI
Ibadan
OSUN

Abeokuta ●

OGUN

Lagos
Badagry ●
LAGOS

ONDO

EDO

Benin City

ANAMBRA

Onitsha ●

Warri
DELTA

Aba ●

Port Harcourt
BAYELSA
RIVERS
Bonny ●
NIGER DELTA

IMO
ABIA

KOGI

ENUGU
● Enugu
EBONYI

CROSS
RIVER
Calabar ●
AKWA
IBOM

Benue
● Makurdi
BENUE

*Kainji
Reservoir*

Sokoto

Hadejia

*Komadougou
Yobe*

14° *Lake
Chad*

Komadougou Gana

Bunga

Gongola

Benue

Niger

Kaduna

Niger

Niger

6°   8°   10°   12°

12°   12°

10°   10°

8°   8°

10°

6°

12°

8°

4°

6°

4°

6°

4°

N

0   100   200 kilometres

0   100   200 miles

Legend
★ Capital
● Cities > 1,000,000
● Cities > 500,000
• Other towns
▲ Mountain
– Dam

CHAPTER 2

History

People have lived in the region now known as Nigeria for at least 11,000 years, and much of Nigeria's early history is actually the separate histories of its different ethnic groups. The earliest evidence of human inhabitants is a skeleton found in south-western Nigeria dating back to around 9000 BC. Other archaeological remains indicate that, around 4,000 years ago, Nigeria was sparsely populated with people who grew crops and kept cattle, goats and sheep. The first organized society in Nigeria was the Nok Culture, which flourished on the Jos Plateau between around 500 BC and AD 200. The Nok people made fine terracotta figurines and probably knew how to work tin and iron.

EMPIRES AND CITY-STATES

Later, between the eighth and nineteenth centuries, several empires and city-states flourished and declined across the region that is modern-day Nigeria. The kingdom of Kanem was the earliest, emerging to the east of Lake Chad some time before AD 900. Traders were drawn to the lake for rest and water as they travelled from North Africa across the Sahara desert. The traders brought Islam to the region, and by the eleventh century the Kanem rulers had all become Muslims. The kingdom of Kanem lost much of its power during the twelfth century but re-emerged to the west of Lake Chad as the Kanem-Bornu empire in the late sixteenth century, following a merger with the Bornu rulers of central Sudan.

◀ The city gates of Kano are one of Nigeria's most important historical structures and a reminder of the former power of the great city-states.

The Kanem-Bornu empire extended its influence as far west as Hausaland in modern-day north and north-central Nigeria. The Hausa are thought to have occupied this area since around the sixth century, and they formed a number of centralized city-states, each of which had grand city walls and a central market. An emir (ruler) controlled each state through a number of chiefs, who, in turn, controlled surrounding villages and collected taxes. Kano, Katsina and Zaria are modern Nigerian cities that began as Hausa city-states.

City-states were also a characteristic of southern Nigeria, where several powerful Yoruba kingdoms vied for power. The first Yoruba city-state was established around the eleventh century at Ife in south-west Nigeria. Benin, Oyo and Ilorin emerged a little later. Between them, they controlled the area from the Niger River to the east and Togo (now an independent country) to the west. The city-states were at their peak in the fifteenth century and became famous for their exquisite ivory, brass and bronze artwork. The Benin kingdom, in particular, left a legacy of beautiful bronze sculptures, known as the Benin Bronzes.

Nigeria's Hausa and Yoruba city-states lost many of their powers after 1804 when Usman Dan Fodio, a Muslim scholar from the Fulani people (a mainly pastoral group from northern Nigeria), launched a series of holy wars (jihads). These wars displaced many of the emirs and created the new caliphate of Sokoto. In south-west Nigeria, the collapse of Oyo led to the Yoruba wars, which lasted until 1886.

▶ A replica of a Benin Bronze. Many of the best original Benin Bronzes were taken by the British and are today housed in the British Museum in London.

THE IGBO

In the south-east, the Igbo civilization can be traced back to at least AD 900. The Igbo lived in small, independent villages, each with its own elected council rather than a chief. Although they traded along the coast, the dense rainforest vegetation, in which they lived, kept them isolated from the rest of the region.

THE ARRIVAL OF THE EUROPEANS

Portuguese traders were the first Europeans to arrive on the Nigerian coast in the late fifteenth century, and they were quickly followed by British, French and Dutch traders. The traders established links with Benin and Oyo to gain riches such as ivory, gold and pepper (a valued spice) but northern kingdoms and city-states were left virtually untouched. Despite Britain's efforts to halt slavery (including outlawing it in 1807), the slave trade continued. It was a highly profitable business for local leaders and slave traders. British forces replaced those local leaders who supported the slave trade and they also tried to police the coast to stop the practice. In 1861, Britain annexed Lagos, claiming it as British territory, so that Britain could use it as a port and to ensure that it was free of slave trading.

Focus on: The slave trade

From the seventeenth to the nineteenth centuries, European traders established coastal ports to transport slaves to South America and the Caribbean. The south-west coast of Nigeria became known as the 'slave coast'. Many people died during violent raids deep into Nigerian territory by merchants looking for slaves. Over 15,000 people were shipped annually from the Bight of Benin and another 15,000 from the Bight of Biafra. In total, up to 30 million slaves may

▲ Local people re-enact the days of slavery in the former slave port town of Badagry, south-west Nigeria, in 2002.

have been sold and transported into slavery from the Nigerian coast. They were sent across the Atlantic Ocean to work on the sugar and cotton plantations of the Caribbean and the southern states of America. The conditions on the ships were appalling and many died on the journey.

COLONIALISM

At a conference in 1884 in Berlin, Germany, the dominant European powers of the time carved up Africa between them. Britain claimed southern Nigeria from the peoples there (mainly the Yoruba and the Igbo), and established control by making treaties with local leaders. Where they encountered resistance, the British used their superior military power to seize control through force.

In the late nineteenth century, Britain began trading in northern Nigeria and negotiated further treaties with local leaders there. By 1900, Britain had gained sufficient control of the region to declare that Nigeria would be administered as two protectorates – the Protectorate of Southern Nigeria and the Protectorate of Northern Nigeria. In 1914, these were joined and Nigeria was created, bringing the region's different peoples together as one political entity. Britain imposed a system called 'indirect rule', in which local leaders were allowed to rule as long as they collected taxes for Britain and complied with what Britain wanted. This succeeded in the Islamic north, where the emirs acted as executors of British policy, but in southern Yorubaland there was more resistance.

Under British rule, most of Nigeria's trade was with Britain. Crops such as palm oil, cotton and groundnuts were grown in large quantities for export to Britain. This forced many farmers to change the crops they grew, reducing those they grew for their own consumption, and damaged their trading links with North Africa and neighbouring coastal states.

INDEPENDENCE AND AFTER

Nigeria gained its independence from Britain on 1 October 1960, following decades of political struggle against colonial rule. This resistance was led mainly by Nigerian politicians who had been educated in the West and by journalists such as Nnamdi Azikiwe and Obafemi Awolowo. It was a long, hard fight, but was bloodless. In contrast, the first few years of independence were characterized by many, sometimes violent, conflicts within and between the different regions and ethnic groups. For example, in February 1964, the Tiv

▲ De Aholu Whenu Menu Toyi I, the present Oba (King) of Badagry, influences the workings of government as well as holding a local court. During the colonial period, the British controlled much of Nigeria by making agreements with local Obas, who ruled on their behalf.

people, who wanted to govern themselves, launched an attack against the local authorities, but it was suppressed by the Nigerian federal army. In 1963, Nigeria became a federal republic made up of three regions, each with a measure of self-government, but the unrest continued. In January 1966, Igbo army officers staged a coup and the country's first military government was established, only to be overthrown by a Hausa coup in July that year.

MILITARY RULE

A series of military governments controlled the country from 1966 to 1999, with the exception of a brief period of civilian rule between 1979 and 1983, when Lieutenant-General Olusegun Obasanjo handed over power to a democratically elected government. General Sani Abacha, one of the country's later military government leaders, was president from 1993 until his sudden death in 1998. His rule was

▼ Supporters cheer, following elections held in December 1959 to prepare Nigeria for independence from the UK on 1 October 1960. Abubakar Tafawa Balewa was elected Prime Minister to lead Nigeria to independence.

marked by serious human rights abuses. Those who criticized his regime – including journalists and human rights activists – were often imprisoned or killed. After protests from the Nigerian people and pressure from the international community, elections were held in 1999 and civilian rule was restored. Olusegun Obasanjo, a former military government leader, became president of the new civilian government in 1999 and was re-elected in 2003.

VIOLENCE

Since independence, Nigeria has regularly experienced violent conflict, including clashes over oil revenues between the federal government and the minority ethnic groups of the oil-rich Niger Delta, disputes over land in the multi-ethnic 'Middle Belt' (the central region of Nigeria), and clashes between Christian and Muslim communities both in the north and in the Middle Belt.

Focus on: The Biafra War

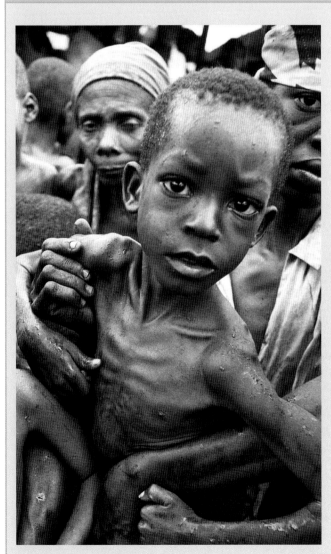

In 1966, the Hausa people of northern Nigeria became especially resentful of the wealthy, better-educated Igbo people who came mainly from the Eastern Region. In September 1966, the Hausa people's increasing resentment led some of them to massacre up to 30,000 Igbo people living in northern Nigeria. Around a million more Igbo fled to the Eastern Region and non-Igbo people were in turn expelled from the Igbo's eastern homelands. The governor of the Eastern Region, Colonel Odumegwu Ojukwu, declared independence from Nigeria in May 1967 and formed the new sovereign state of Biafra. But fighting broke out between Nigerian federal forces and those of Biafra. The conflict was one of Africa's bloodiest civil wars, in which several million people may have died. Many Biafrans died of starvation because the Nigerian forces cut off the supply routes into Biafra. By January 1970, Nigerian military gains and a starving population forced the Biafran leaders into exile. Biafra ceased to exist on 15 January 1970 and the region again became part of Nigeria.

◀ The images of famine from Biafra shocked people all over the world in the late 1960s.

CHAPTER 3

Landscape and Climate

Nigeria covers an area of 923,768 sq km (356,667 sq miles) – slightly more than twice the size of California, and three times the size of the UK. It has a wide range of different landscapes, from swamps and deserts to mountains and plains. The country's two main rivers, the Niger and the Benue, meet to the south of the centre of Nigeria, forming a 'Y' shape.

LANDSCAPE

Washed by the Atlantic Ocean, the south coast of Nigeria is a low-lying area of sandy beaches, lagoons and mangrove swamps. To the east, the coastline is broken by the huge delta of the River Niger. The coastal plain, with its sedimentary rocks, extends some 10 km (6 miles) inland, from where a tract of rainforest gradually rises towards the Middle Belt. In eastern Nigeria, on its borders with Cameroon, lie the Central Highlands and Chappal Waddi, Nigeria's highest point at 2,419 m (7,936 feet).

▼ Rainforest vegetation once covered much of southern Nigeria, but is today limited to a few remaining areas such as part of Cross River State.

The Middle Belt, north of the coastal plain, has an average altitude of around 700 m (2,300 feet). Isolated areas on the Jos Plateau, part of the Central Plateau, reach 1,200 m (3,900 feet). The Central Plateau is an area of savannah grasslands and open woodland, with a few isolated areas of volcanic and igneous rocks, such as granite, that form dramatic, beautiful scenery with waterfalls and rock pools.

The northern half of Nigeria is made up of ancient crystalline rocks that have been weathered and eroded over millions of years, forming broad, level plateau land, with low granite hills, or inselbergs. From these plateau lands, the altitude falls to the low-lying Chad and Sokoto basins in the far north-east and north-west. The northernmost part of this area is mainly desert and semi-desert and marks the southern edge of the Sahara desert.

▲ A villager passes along a path that crosses the granite hills (inselbergs) that typify the Jos Plateau area around the city of Jos.

CLIMATE

Nigeria's climate is equatorial in the south, tropical in the centre, and semi-arid in the north. Temperatures are generally high all year round, usually over 30°C (86°F), with the highest temperatures towards the end of the dry season. The main climatic variable for the whole country is rainfall, which is controlled by two air masses – moist, northward-moving, maritime air coming from the Atlantic Ocean and dry continental air moving south from the Sahara desert. These air currents meet in the Inter-Tropical Convergence Zone (ITCZ), and it is their seasonal movement that dictates Nigeria's, and, indeed, much of Africa's rainfall pattern.

▲ Men fishing in one of the mangrove creeks of the Niger Delta.

The south, with its equatorial climate, is hot and rainy most of the year, with a relatively dry period between November and March. The rainy season usually begins in February as moist Atlantic air arrives. The highest rainfall is along the south-east coast, particularly around Bonny where average annual rainfall is more than 4,000 mm (157 inches). Most of the south-east receives 2,000-3,000 mm (79-118 inches) a year. In the south-west, there is often a decrease in rainfall in August, allowing a brief dry period during which grain is harvested.

Focus on: The Niger Delta

The Niger Delta protrudes into the Gulf of Guinea. It covers an area of approximately 14,000 sq km (5,400 sq miles) and is made up of swampland, intricate networks of creeks and lagoons, mangroves and numerous small islands. It drains a catchment area of over a million square kilometres and is one of the largest delta systems in the world. Oil formed in this region millions of years ago from the fossils of tiny sea creatures and plants that accumulated on the seabed. The Niger Delta is the home of many different ethnic groups and has been extensively exploited for its oil.

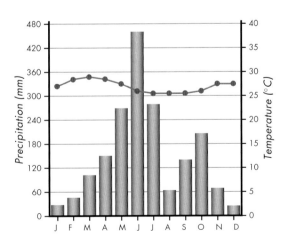

▲ Average monthly climate conditions in Lagos

The central area and the north have a tropical climate, becoming semi-arid in the far north. There are two main seasons – the long dry season from October to May and the short rainy season from June to September. The rains can be heavy and frequently result in flash floods. The north is drier than the south, and it is possible to have five months here with no rain.

The greatest extremes of temperature are found in the north-east. Here, temperatures often reach as high as 44°C (111°F) before the onset of the rains, or drop as low as 6°C (43°F) during the occasional intrusion of cool air from the north between December and February.

In the dry season, the sky is often laden with sand and dust from the Sahara brought in by the north-east trade winds, known locally as the Harmattan. These winds can be felt as far south as Lagos.

Did you know?

In June 2002, more than 60 people died of heat stroke in the north-eastern city of Maiduguri when temperatures reached 55°C (130°F).

Focus on: Climate change

Frequent droughts occurred in Nigeria during the 1970s and 1980s, particularly in the north, leading to crop failure and famine. Experts consider it to have been one of the driest periods in centuries and they have speculated that the dryness might be a sign of climate change.

In 2005 the Nigerian High Court ruled that the flaring or burning of natural gas in the oil fields of the Niger Delta was against the law. This reflected the government's aim to reduce the potential impact of climate change. Gas flaring produces large quantities of carbon dioxide and methane – two of the gases that have been linked to the process of climate change. Gas vapours are a by-product of oil drilling, and they are flared in order to dispose of them. In 2003, Nigeria accounted for about 12.5 per cent of the world's gas flaring.

▼ Gas flaring from an oil well in the Niger Delta region. There is concern about how much this practice contributes to climate change.

CHAPTER 4

Population and Settlements

In 2008, Nigeria had an estimated 145 million people, making it by far the largest population in Africa. Nigeria also has one of the fastest-growing populations in Africa, and indeed the world. In the period 2000-2005, the annual population growth rate was 2.5 per cent, compared to an African average of 2.2 per cent each year and a world average of 1.2 per cent each year. Experts predict that population growth will begin to slow in Nigeria, but it is still expected to be around 2.3 per cent each year for the period 2000-2015.

Children are highly valued in Nigerian society, as most parents believe that their children will look after them when they are elderly – an important consideration in a country that has limited social welfare services. As a result, Nigerian families are generally very large.

The average Nigerian woman gives birth at least five times in her lifetime, although women who are better educated generally tend to have fewer children.

But this level of growth is unsustainable both for Nigeria and for the individual families, many of whom live in poverty. The country's population growth has severe consequences for the quality of life of all Nigerians because it puts a huge strain on the country's services, including water supplies, housing, health and education.

With poverty and a lack of basic healthcare comes a high mortality rate. In 2006, for every 1,000 children born, 191 died before reaching

Population data

- Population: 144.7 million
- Population 0-14 yrs: 44%
- Population 15-64 yrs: 53%
- Population 65+ yrs: 3%
- Population growth rate (2000-2005): 2.35%
- Population density:158.9 per sq km/405.7 per sq mile
- Urban population: 49%
- Major cities: Lagos 11,135,000, Kano 2,884,000, Ibadan 2,375,000

Sources: United Nations and World Bank

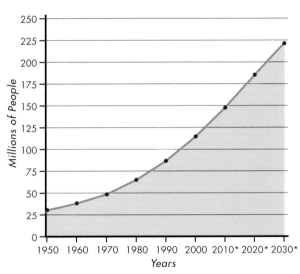

* Projected Population

▲ Population growth, 1950-2030

▲ Over 40 per cent of Nigeria's population is under 14 years of age.

the age of five, and life expectancy at birth was just 46 years for men and 47 years for women. Another factor that is having an increasing impact on Nigeria's population is HIV/AIDS. By 2003, it was estimated that 4.6 per cent of men and 6.2 per cent of women between the ages of 15 and 49 were living with HIV/AIDS. Worryingly, some health experts believe this proportion could double by the year 2010.

Did you know?

In 2004, Nigeria was the tenth most populous country in the world.

Focus on: The census

Though the size of Nigeria's population can be estimated, its precise size is harder to ascertain. A census was held in 1991 but the results were contested by rival regions and ethnic groups. The problem is that whichever ethnic group turns out to be the largest ends up with a greater share of power in government because seats in the House of Representatives are allocated on the basis of population size. Taking a census is therefore very controversial and the government frequently puts it off, saying that it could cause conflict and violence. (If it were found that the leaders were not from the dominant group, the census result could challenge their position of power.) A census in 2006 showed that the population was around 140 million.

POPULATION DENSITY

Nigeria had an average population density in 2006 of 158.9 people per sq km (405.7 people per square mile) but distribution is not even throughout the country. The south is more densely populated, with 500-1,000 people per square kilometre. Even in rural areas, population density can be as high as 400. In semi-arid parts of the north, population density is often very low, but there are high concentrations of people in and around urban areas such as Kano and Sokoto.

MIGRATION TO THE CITIES

Rural poverty and a lack of job opportunities have forced many young people to move to the cities. It is fairly common to find villages where most of the young, able-bodied men have gone to the cities, leaving women to do the farming

and take care of children and the elderly. In some cases, this migration has led to the complete abandonment of farms.

Nigeria has experienced rapid urbanization, with over 49 per cent of its population living in towns and cities as of 2006, up from just 15.2 per cent at independence in 1960. The urban population is expected to continue increasing to reach around 65 per cent of the total population by 2030. Most urban centres in Nigeria are small to medium in size, with only 11 having a population of over 750,000 in 2007. Whatever their size, most have

▼ A Hausa/Fulani homestead in northern Nigeria. The north of Nigeria is more sparsely populated and more rural than the south of the country.

grown at an extraordinary rate, with little urban planning. This has resulted in massive problems of traffic congestion, poor housing, and inadequate waste management and water supplies (presenting considerable health risks). Air pollution is also a problem and is caused by the burning of waste, the use of wood and charcoal for cooking, and emissions from poor-quality vehicles on crowded roads.

▲ A dense urban neighbourhood in Kano, Nigeria's second-largest city. It consists of mainly low-quality housing and is typical of Nigeria's urban centres.

Did you know?

Nigeria covers 15 per cent of the land area of West Africa but has 52 per cent of its people.

Focus on: Lagos

When Nigeria won its independence in 1960, the then capital, Lagos, had a population of just 762,000. By 2005, Lagos's population had grown to 8.8 million, and is expected to reach 10.6 million by 2010. This will make it one of only twenty mega-cities (those with over 10 million people). By 2020, the United Nations predicts that its population will top 14.1 million and make Lagos the twelfth most populous city in the world. Besides being by far Nigeria's largest city, Lagos is also its leading port and an important centre of intellectual and cultural life, with several universities and colleges, the National Library and the National Museum. However, Lagos compares badly with cities in other parts of the world in terms of quality of life, with many of its houses being no more than makeshift huts on unpaved roads and with no services. The city does, however, have pockets of good housing and apartment buildings where Lagos's rich and the majority of the expatriate community live. Homes in these more desirable areas of the city have become fortresses in order to guard against crime.

CHAPTER 5

Government and Politics

Nigeria gained its independence in 1960, but the country has been in political turmoil virtually ever since, with its numerous military governments oppressing – and sometimes assassinating – their political rivals. However, since 1999, with a return to democratic civilian rule, the country's government has become much more stable, and many Nigerians are optimistic about the future.

NIGERIA'S FEDERAL SYSTEM

Nigeria became a federal republic in 1963 and is today made up of 36 states and the federal capital territory at Abuja. National laws and decisions on issues such as defence and foreign affairs are made by the central government, while each state has a large degree of autonomous rule and can make state laws. In northern Nigeria, several predominantly Islamic states have adopted Sharia law, or Islamic law, as their state legal system.

Nigeria's president presides over a parliamentary government consisting of two chambers. The upper chamber (the Senate) contains 109 seats, three for each of Nigeria's 36 states and one seat for the federal capital territory. The lower chamber, or House of Representatives, contains 360 seats and is made up of 10 seats for each state. The country's president and members of both chambers of parliament are elected for four-year terms.

The federal system is particularly important in Nigeria because it allows the country's diverse ethnic and religious groups to be governed in ways that are appropriate to them. To some extent, it also helps balance the power between the country's leading ethnic groups – the Hausa

◀ Posters of the current president, here Olusegun Obasanjo, appear all over Nigeria. In 2007 President Obasanjo nominated Umaru Yar'Adua to succeed him.

and Fulani in the north, the Yoruba in the south-west and the Igbo in the south-east. The Nigerian federal system does not always run smoothly, however, and disputes between central government and individual states are common, particularly over the allocation of national resources.

▼ A meeting of the chiefs of Badagry (local traditional governors), who still make decisions on many local issues.

MOVING THE CAPITAL

Until 1976, the mainly Yoruba city of Lagos in the south was the capital of Nigeria. However, in that year, the capital was moved to the new city of Abuja, located just north of the point at which the Niger and Benue rivers meet, almost in the centre of the country. It was thought that the relocation of the capital, to a place between the main north and south ethnic blocs, would help to balance political power between the regions and help to calm the tensions between them.

RETURN TO CIVILIAN RULE

After years of condemnation by the international community for the country's lack of democracy and its disregard for human rights, the country's military leader, General Abdulsalam Abubakar, voluntarily stepped down in 1999, and Nigeria returned to civilian rule and democracy. A new constitution was also adopted in 1999, guaranteeing Nigerians freedom of expression and religion and prohibiting discrimination on grounds of ethnicity, religion, gender or place of origin. With the introduction of these reforms, sanctions that had previously been imposed by the international community against Nigeria, were dropped. Nigeria has managed to maintain a democratic civilian government into the early twenty-first century, but allegations of corruption and problems caused by the slow pace of change still plague its political leaders. However, the international community continues to support the transition to civilian rule, hoping to avoid a return to Nigeria's turbulent past. In February 2005, for example, the European Union pledged funds to help Nigeria conduct a full population census – the first since its return to democracy.

Focus on: Controversy over Sharia

Nigeria's national legal system is based on the English system, but in 2000, a number of largely Muslim states in the north adopted Sharia, which is a body of Islamic law. Sharia is used in both civil and criminal cases, but its laws sometimes conflict with federal laws, as in the case of Amina Lawal. In 2002, the Sharia court of Katsina State sentenced Lawal to be stoned to death for having given birth outside marriage. This sentence was much harsher than any that would have been given under the federal law and sparked protests both within and beyond Nigeria. The Sharia Court of Appeal later quashed the sentence and Amina Lawal was released, but her case highlighted the controversy over the acceptance of Sharia in the north of Nigeria. Although Sharia law does not apply to non-Muslims, many non-Muslims living in the north object to it being adopted as a legal

▲ Amina Lawal, with her baby and her father.

system in their states. There have been several violent clashes between Muslims and non-Muslims since the Sharia system has been adopted in Nigeria's northern states. In total, more than 10,000 people have died in these violent confrontations.

Despite a number of delays and problems, the census was successfully carried out in 2006.

UNREST CONTINUES

The return to civilian rule and the lifting of sanctions has not stopped the unrest and often violent demonstrations. The people of the Niger Delta, for example, mount protests, claiming that oil companies are damaging their environment and that very little of the money earned from oil is used to benefit Delta communities. Government corruption at all levels also remains widespread and undermines people's faith in the democratic process. Holding office in the government is seen by many as a way for individuals to benefit themselves or members of their own families, while the problems of growing poverty and poor infrastructure continue for the majority.

Focus on: Nigeria's human rights record

Since the death of the former military leader, General Abacha, in June 1998, Nigeria's human rights record has improved considerably. Military decrees allowing people to be detained and put on trial for no apparent reason have been revoked. However, prison conditions are still very poor, and corruption, particularly at high levels, continues to be a big problem. Democracy may have been restored, but there are still human rights violations such as police torture and corruption in the judiciary. And, even today, the Nigerian government does not easily tolerate those who criticize it. In May 2004, for example, Nigerian novelist Wole Soyinka was arrested after taking part in a demonstration against the government because he believed that it had failed to restore civil rights quickly enough after the country had returned to civilian rule.

▶ Wole Soyinka speaks about the problem of violence in Nigeria in 2002. As a particularly outspoken Nigerian, he has frequently found himself in trouble with the authorities.

CHAPTER 6

Energy and Resources

Nigeria has many minerals, such as iron ore, and energy resources, including oil and natural gas. Land and water are also important resources, with about half the country's land suitable for farming or grazing, and lakes, rivers and streams providing abundant fish.

▼ Even though Nigeria is a major oil producer, fuel is scarce and expensive, and people often have to buy it on the black market, from roadside sellers like the ones shown here.

ENERGY SOURCES

Ever since its discovery in the 1950s, oil has been at the heart of Nigeria's politics and its economy. In 2007, Nigeria was the world's thirteenth-biggest oil producer, providing 3.1 per cent of the world total. Most of Nigeria's oil is found in the shallow waters of the Niger Delta, but offshore deposits have also been discovered and deep-sea fields are being explored. Nigeria has five state-controlled oil refineries but these do not produce enough refined oil to meet the country's needs. In 2007, Nigeria's four main refineries had the ability to produce 439 billion barrels per day of refined petroleum but poor maintenance meant that only 50 per cent of that total was produced. The government is proposing to build new refineries. This will provide new jobs and reduce the need for Nigeria to import refined oil products.

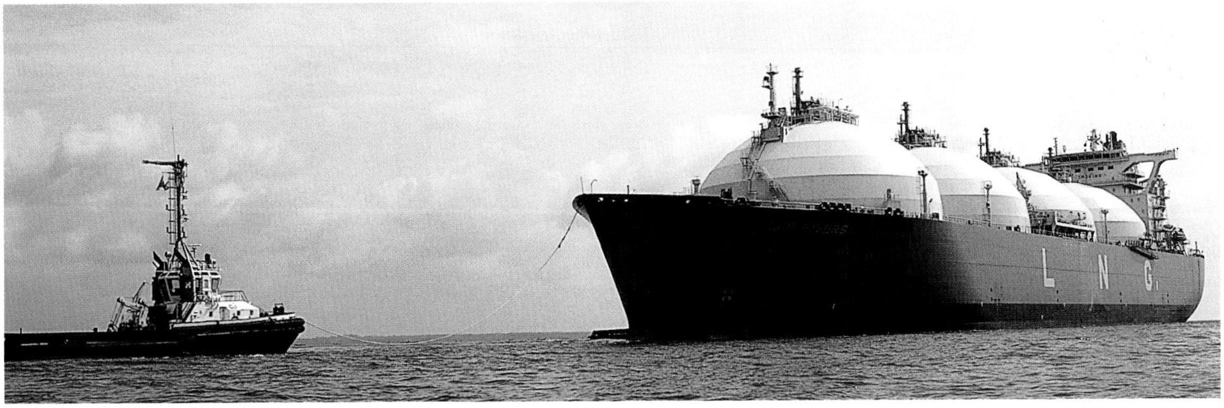
L N G

▲ A tanker carrying liquid natural gas (LNG). LNG is a valuable addition to Nigeria's fuel portfolio because it is in growing demand all over the world.

Vast natural gas reserves, estimated at 5 trillion cubic metres (176.5 trillion cubic feet) in 2006, or 2.8 per cent of the world total, have been found in the Niger Delta region. But a lack of investment means they are only being partly exploited. Not surprisingly, foreign investors have been unwilling to invest in Nigeria's gas industry until they are sure of the country's stability. In 2006 natural gas production was five times as high as in 1999, showing that the new civilian government was building confidence. In 2006, the Nigerian High Court ruled that the wasteful practice of flaring (burning) natural gas by-products from oil extraction was illegal. There are plans to convert the waste gas into liquid natural gas (LNG) for domestic use and export, and to construct a West African Gas Pipeline to supply Nigerian gas to Benin, Togo and Ghana.

ENERGY USE

Between 1980 and 2005, Nigeria's annual energy consumption doubled and it is currently increasing by 2 to 5 per cent a year. However, in relation to other major African nations, energy consumption remains

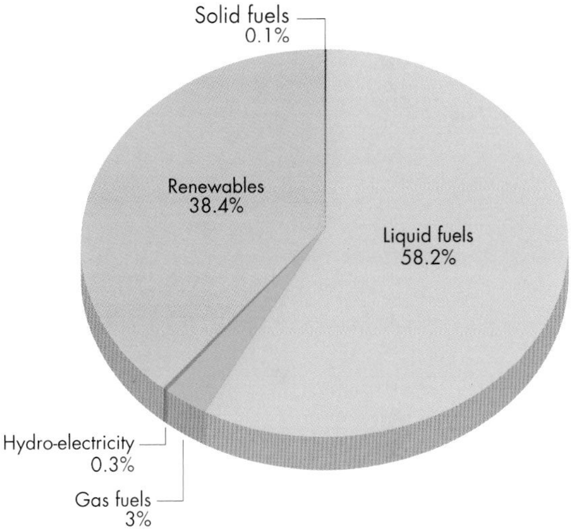
Solid fuels
0.1%
Renewables
38.4%
Liquid fuels
58.2%
Hydro-electricity
0.3%
Gas fuels
3%

▲ Energy use by type

Energy data

- Energy consumption as % of world total: 2.0
- Energy consumption by sector (% of total)
  Industry: 11, Transportation: 7, Agriculture: 0
  Services: 1, Residential: 81
- CO_2 emissions as % of world total: 0.4
- CO_2 emissions per capita p.a.: 0.7 tonnes (0.69 tons)

Source: World Resources Institute

▲ Like many Nigerians, this young boy regularly gathers wood for use as bio-fuel.

low in Nigeria, at less than half that of Egypt and less than a quarter that of South Africa. One reason for Nigeria's low energy consumption is that, by 2004, only around 40 per cent of Nigerians had access to electricity.

Nigeria has eight electricity generating stations throughout the country, including five thermal power stations which use oil and gas, and three hydro-electric power (HEP) plants, located at Kainji, Jebba and Shiroro. Electricity generated by HEP has more than doubled since 1980 but unreliable rainfall means that reservoir levels frequently fall, resulting in disruptive power cuts. Nevertheless, the government intends to increase production of HEP and, in 2003, approved the construction of a US$ 6 billion HEP project on the Mambila Plateau in north-east Nigeria. This plant will produce 3,960 megawatts (MW) when completed, a significant proportion of Nigeria's 2004 total electricity capacity of 5,900 MW.

Focus on: Bio-fuels

Despite living in a country rich in fossil fuels, most Nigerians rely on bio-fuels, such as wood, charcoal, dried vegetation and combustible waste (paper, card, etc) as their main energy sources. In 2001, such fuels accounted for around 78 per cent of Nigeria's total energy use. In principle, the use of bio-fuels is sustainable, if trees are replanted faster than they are cleared.

 Did you know?

If Nigeria continues to produce oil at current rates, it has enough proven reserves to keep producing until around 2050.

MINERAL RESOURCES

Nigeria's mineral deposits include iron ore, tin, columbite (used in making stainless steel), coal, limestone, gypsum, bauxite, lead, titanium, marble, gold and zinc. Tin and columbite are found on the Jos Plateau, and limestone, which is important for the iron and steel industry, is found in the valleys of the Niger, Benue and Sokoto rivers.

Much of Nigeria's mineral wealth remains unexploited because of lack of investment. The states of Kogi, Enugu and Niger, for instance, are thought to possess over 3 billion tonnes (2.95 billion tons) of iron ore deposits, but Nigeria imports iron ore for use in its steel industry. Bauxite, the main raw material for aluminium, has been found on the Mambila and Jos Plateaus. The government hopes to use this to develop the aluminium industry, if capital is forthcoming from investors.

FARMING, FORESTRY AND FISHING

Nigeria's people still largely depend upon the country's land and waters for their living. Over 60 per cent of the population is involved in subsistence agriculture, producing food crops such as sorghum and millet in the north and yams and cassava in the south. Nigeria's main cash crops, or crops grown for export, include cocoa, palm oil, groundnuts and cotton. Forest products are also exported, though the government is now imposing limits on forestry to protect Nigeria's remaining rainforests.

Most of Nigeria's lakes and rivers provide fish for local people or for sale in urban markets, but the country's main sources of fish are Lake Chad and Lake Kainji in the north and the Niger Delta in the south. In most parts of Nigeria, fishing is a small-scale industry using traditional methods, but over-fishing to meet the needs of a growing population is a concern in some areas. Atlantic fisheries provide income and employment for many coastal Nigerians. But their livelihoods are threatened by large, unregulated trawlers (some from other West African countries and some from Japan, Korea and Spain) that are able to catch huge numbers of fish, thus depleting the stocks left for the locals. The government has imposed restrictions on trawlers – they are not allowed to fish at depths of less than 20 m (65 feet) or less than 5 km (3 miles) from the shoreline – but these regulations are not always respected.

▲ Tin-mining on the Jos Plateau is no longer commercially viable but many small-scale miners continue to extract tin from the area as a way of boosting their incomes.

CHAPTER 7

Economy and Income

Nigeria traditionally had an agricultural economy, but the discovery of oil (and later gas) radically changed the make-up of its economy. In the 1970s, when global oil prices were particularly high, Nigeria had the fastest-

▼ This view of Lagos, with its skyscrapers, shows where much of Nigeria's oil revenue has been spent.

growing economy in Africa. For more than a decade, over US$100 billion of oil revenue poured in. It was more money, in less time, than any nation in sub-Saharan Africa had ever seen. For a while, Nigeria's economy looked set to grow and grow.

SPEND, SPEND, SPEND

In reality, most of the oil revenue was spent on expensive projects, that mainly benefited the rich elite, such as a vast highway system and

more than twenty new universities. Little of the money trickled down to ordinary Nigerians and few of these projects did anything to relieve the problems of the poor. Despite Nigeria's apparent wealth, the government took out huge loans to develop its grand projects, believing that unlimited oil revenue would allow them to repay the loans. And then, in the mid-1980s, the price of oil plummeted and Nigeria's economic boom fizzled out. Nigeria was unable to repay its loans and saw its debts increase from US$9

billion in 1980 to US$33 billion by 1989. In 2005, Nigeria still owed at least US$22 billion and, unless international organizations and governments cancel it, the debt will increase each year as the interest mounts up. Today, money that is needed to provide basic services like education and health (including drugs to treat HIV/AIDS), and to build a stronger, more varied economy, is used for interest repayments instead.

▲ Life is hard in this Ogoni village in the Niger Delta. The Ogoni people suffer poverty and deprivation, and have benefited little from the oil found on their land.

 Did you know?

About 70 per cent of Nigerians were living on less than US$1 per day in 2005 and 90 per cent were surviving on less than US$2.

Focus on: Oil dependency

Hydrocarbons (oil and natural gas) accounted for 90-95 per cent of Nigeria's export earnings in 2006. In the past, the military rulers failed to diversify the economy and the country became over-dependent on hydrocarbons, especially oil. In 2003, for example, oil provided 20 per cent of Nigeria's Gross Domestic Product (GDP), 90 per cent of its foreign exchange earnings, and up to 80 per cent of government revenues. Being so dependent on oil has made Nigeria extremely vulnerable to changes in oil prices on the world market. Between 1998 and 2007, for instance, the price of a barrel of Nigerian crude oil varied from a low of US$12.62 to a high of US$74.48.

When the price is low, Nigeria has little to fall back on. However, by joining OPEC (the Organization of Petroleum Exporting Countries) in 1971, Nigeria gained some ability to influence world prices. OPEC members meet regularly to agree on production levels in an attempt to affect world oil supplies and therefore prices. OPEC has become less influential in recent years because of the emergence of new non-OPEC suppliers such as Russia and China. For this reason, Nigeria can no longer rely on OPEC to protect its oil revenues. Instead, Nigeria needs to reduce its dependence on oil and find new ways of diversifying its economy.

POVERTY AND INEQUALITY

The mismanagement of Nigeria's oil revenue has been widely blamed for the country's high rates of poverty. In 2003, the average Gross National Income (GNI) per person was just US$320, although by 2007 this had risen to US$930. Inequality is also a problem. In 2003 (the last year for which data was collected), the wealthiest 10 per cent of the population enjoyed one third of Nigeria's income. By contrast, the poorest 10 per cent shared just 1.9 per cent of the national income.

▼ A pastoralist in northern Nigeria herds his goats. There are many others like him, who depend on the land for their living.

ECONOMIC STRUCTURE

Over 60 per cent of Nigerians still live and work in farming villages. Most of them work the land, producing food crops for their own use, and selling any surplus at markets. In addition to farming, many people have other jobs, such as producing crafts or doing repair work.

Until the 1970s, Nigeria used to be an exporter of food. During the boom years of the 1970s, however, the Nigerian government imported food. This undermined local farming because the imported goods were often cheaper. People moved to the cities from the countryside in search of jobs, and farming suffered. In the year 2004, agriculture accounted for only 20 per cent of the total value of Nigeria's production, whereas oil accounted for as much as 70 per cent.

Economic data

📁 Gross National Income (GNI) in US$: 137,091,000,000
📁 World rank by GNI: 45
📁 GNI per capita in US$: 930
📁 World rank by GNI per capita: 161
Economic growth: 5%
Source: World Bank

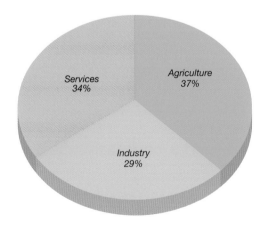

Services 34%

Agriculture 37%

Industry 29%

▲ Contribution by sector to national income

▲ This Nigerian woman works in the service sector, selling mobile phones.

In 1999, around 10 per cent of the workforce was involved in manufacturing industries, such as steel, pulp and paper, cloth and textiles, processed food, cement and beer, and 20 per cent worked in service industries, such as banking and transport. Service industries are becoming more important, and in 2002, they accounted for 34 per cent of the country's GDP. There has been some growth, particularly in banking and the civil service. Women are increasingly involved in the job market and a few Nigerian women are now qualifying as doctors, engineers and bankers.

UNEMPLOYMENT

Unemployment has been a problem in Nigeria since the 1980s. It is difficult to calculate the exact number of people without jobs, but in 2007 it was estimated that 68 million were

unemployed, mainly in the cities. In rural areas, people are given food and shelter by their families and are likely to be under-employed rather than unemployed. In other words, they have work but not enough to bring in a living wage.

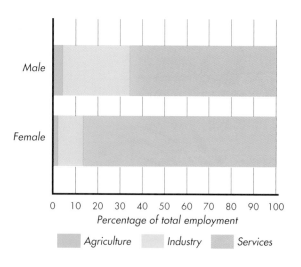

▲ Labour force by sector and gender

CHAPTER 8

Global Connections

For over 700 years, Nigeria has had strong links with other countries, mainly through trade. Nigeria's connections with the rest of the world have grown since it became independent in 1960.

NIGERIA AND AFRICA

Despite its difficulties at home, Nigeria has continued to play a prominent role in West Africa, where its relative wealth and large population make it the leading nation in the region. It was a founding member of the Economic Community of West African States (ECOWAS), which was established in 1975 to promote trade, co-operation and self-reliance among West African states. Nigeria provided a peacekeeping force for the ECOWAS Ceasefire Monitoring Group (ECOMOG) when it contributed 900 personnel in August 1990 to serve in trouble spots throughout West Africa. In particular, Nigerian soldiers formed the basis of the ECOMOG peacekeeping force during the 11-year war in Sierra Leone, which started in the early 1990s. However, Nigeria had to withdraw its troops in 2000, as it could no longer afford the US$1 million it was spending each day on peace enforcement there.

◄ Former Nigerian president (1999-2007), Olusegun Obasanjo, addresses the United Nations in New York, in 2004.

NIGERIA'S ROLE IN THE WORLD

When it became independent in 1960, Nigeria joined the United Nations and the Commonwealth (a voluntary association of 53 independent states, which, apart from Mozambique, have experienced – directly or indirectly – British rule), and Nigeria hosted the Heads of Commonwealth meeting in 2003. Along with South Africa, Nigeria is a leading voice within Africa. It condemned apartheid in South Africa and has argued for Africa to have a permanent place on the United Nations Security Council. Nigeria would like an African country – itself, South Africa or Egypt – to join the five permanent members of the Security Council (Britain, China, France, Russia and the United States) to ensure a better representation of African interests within the United Nations. The Security Council is the United Nations' most powerful body and works to maintain international peace and security.

Focus on: Nigeria, the African Union and the Darfur crisis

Nigeria plays a leading role in the African Union, which replaced the Organization of African Unity in 2002. The African Union aims to promote peace across the African continent. In August 2004, the Nigerian president, Olusegun Obasanjo, hosted talks to resolve the conflict in the Darfur region of the Sudan, where civil war had led to the deaths of thousands of people. The Darfur revolt broke out in early 2003, after years of conflict between Arab nomads and African farmers over scarce resources in the arid, landlocked region. President Obasanjo urged the deployment of African Union forces to help restore peace there.

▼ Nigerian Major-General Festus Okonkwo, chairman of the African Union mission in western Sudan's troubled Darfur region, inspects Rwandan troops in November 2004.

Nigeria has strategic importance as one of the world's major oil producers and is a member of the Organization of Petroleum Exporting Countries (OPEC), which sets levels of output among its member states. OPEC influences global supply and, therefore, the price of oil. Nigeria is the United States' second-biggest trading partner in Africa, after South Africa. It is also a member of the World Trade Organization, which gives it the advantage of access to wider global markets.

▼ US President George W. Bush stands with former Nigerian President Olusegun Obasanjo at a summit in Abuja in 2003. The summit was held to consider closer economic ties between the USA and Nigeria and other African countries.

With its large population, and the possibility of increased prosperity in the future, Nigeria could become a sizeable market for goods from elsewhere, providing further trade opportunities for manufacturers and producers from North America, Europe and the rest of Africa.

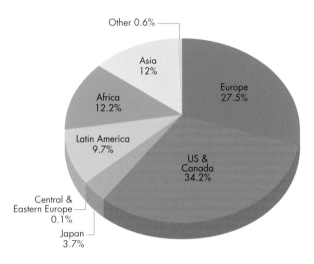

▲ Destination of exports by major trading region

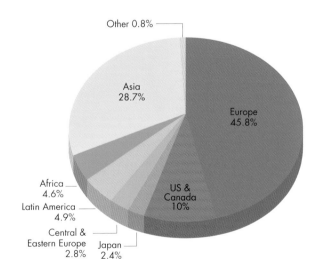

▲ Origin of imports by major trading region

NIGERIA AND THE ARTS

Nigeria's connections with the rest of the world extend beyond the political and the economic. In particular, it has had a big influence in the arts. In the seventeenth and eighteenth centuries, Nigerian slaves carried their tradition of oral storytelling to the Caribbean, Latin America and the United States, and Nigerian folktales and literature are known around the world. Particularly well known are the stories of Anancy the Spider. Nigeria's modern literature has been highly praised internationally, and Nigerians have won many awards. Nigerian novelist Wole Soyinka won the Nobel Prize for Literature in 1986, and in 1991 Ben Okri, another Nigerian novelist, won the Booker Prize for *The Famished Road*.

The movement of people out of Nigeria has also taken the influence of African music to many different parts of the world. Jazz is partly based on African techniques of interweaving rhythm and melodies, and call-and-response patterns. African music was taken to the United States, Cuba and Brazil by slaves, where it contributed to the development of jazz, blues and modern popular music. Calypso was heavily influenced by African work songs and the xylophone originated in this part of Africa.

> **Did you know?**
>
> Many early twentieth-century European artists, such as Pablo Picasso, Henri Matisse and Amedeo Modigliani, were influenced by wooden statues and masks from Nigeria.

▶ Traditional Nigerian masks, like this one, influenced some of the paintings of Pablo Picasso.

Focus on: The Nigerian diaspora

Thousands of people have left Nigeria in search of work because the country's economic problems have led to a great deal of unemployment. At least 100,000 Nigerian professionals are currently working in the United States. There are also significant Nigerian communities in the UK, Canada, Saudi Arabia and, increasingly, in South Africa. Since the 1970s, this large-scale emigration is thought to have cost the Nigerian economy around US$100 billion.

CHAPTER 9

Transport and Communications

Although Nigeria's transport infrastructure was improved in the 1970s and 1980s, it has since fallen into disrepair and this has had a bad effect on businesses, which need to transport their goods around the country. When the new government took power in 1999, it was faced with a chaotic transport system, and it decided to make improving transport a priority.

ROAD AND RAIL

Poorly maintained roads are a particular problem during Nigeria's rainy season. Heavy downpours can create dangerous potholes in paved roads and sometimes even wash the roads away, making some rural areas inaccessible by car. Most Nigerians travel by bus or taxi, both between and within cities. The use of motorcycles and motor scooters, as well as bicycles, is more common in the north, where there is more poverty. In cities, many people travel in dilapidated, privately owned minibuses (known as *danfos*) and overcrowded buses (known as *molues*). Nigerian

▼ Traffic congestion in Lagos.

city roads are very congested and Nigerians refer to traffic jams as 'go-slows'. Victoria Island, on which the central business district of Lagos is built and which has a particularly bad reputation for congestion, is connected to the mainland by a fly-over which is commonly known as the 'crawl-over' because the traffic moves so slowly over it.

Nigeria's railway network was built by the British primarily to transport goods to the ports for export. There are about 3,557 km (2,209 miles) of railway but years of neglect have reduced the usefulness of both the rolling stock and the track. By 2004, for example, only around 15 per cent of Nigeria's 200 or so locomotives were in good working order. Concerned about the decline of what was once Africa's greatest railway network, the Nigerian government announced a US$60 billion plan to restore the railways over the next 25 years. By February 2005, the first concessions (business agreements) were being set up to allow private companies to invest in and operate elements of the railway system. It is hoped that private investment from the sale of such concessions will help to kick-start the rebuilding process.

▲ Roads can often become impassable during the rainy season.

RIVER TRANSPORT

In the past, the River Niger was important for freight traffic, particularly during the colonial era. In the nineteenth century, British companies were operating vessels far inland. River transport played a part in the development of the timber industry and in the establishment of oil-palm and rubber-tree plantations.

 Did you know?

Nigeria has one of the highest road accident rates in the world. In Lagos, on average, one person is killed in a car accident every day.

Transport & communications data

- Total roads: 193,200 km/120,049 miles
- Total paved roads: 60,068 km/37,325 miles
- Total unpaved roads: 134,326 km/83,466 miles
- Total railways: 3,505 km/2,178 miles
- Airports: 36
- Cars per 1,000 people: 8
- Mobile phones per 1,000 people: 223
- Personal computers per 1,000 people: 80
- Internet users per 1,000 people: 55

Sources: World Bank and CIA World Factbook

Nigeria has over 3,000 km (1,875 miles) of potentially navigable inland waterways. In the late 1980s, a number of river ports were upgraded, and locks were constructed at Kainji dam to allow ships to travel further upstream. There has been renewed interest in river transport because it is a cheap, safe and environmentally friendly mode of transportation. In 1999, a project was started in the Lower Niger River to dredge and maintain a navigation channel of about 573 km (358 miles) from Baro to Warri.

MASS MEDIA COMMUNICATIONS

Successive Nigerian governments have claimed that they respect the freedom of the media. Nevertheless, journalists, broadcasters and writers have been arrested and imprisoned for publishing stories that are critical of the government.

With 32 channels, the Nigerian National Television Authority is the largest TV station in sub-Saharan Africa, based on the size of the area covered by its network. There are nine privately owned TV stations in the country. Muslim TV services started up in 2001 in northern Nigeria, broadcasting both religious and political programmes. In September 2003, Nigeria launched its own satellite from Russia, which will eventually be used as a communications satellite. Nigerians who have satellite dishes or cable television often watch CNN, the BBC, and Movie Magic or Supersport from South Africa.

Many Nigerians are keen newspaper readers. Most newspapers are published in English but some are in local Nigerian languages, especially Yoruba and Hausa. Most of the radio stations in Nigeria are government-owned and broadcast in many different languages. There are also private radio stations such as Cool FM. Nigeria has an international radio station – Voice of Nigeria – that broadcasts across West Africa on short wave, and Nigerians also use Voice of America and the BBC World Service as important sources of news.

◀ Newspapers are a very important source of information in a country where television ownership is still minimal. Nigeria has an active press and there are numerous national and regional papers.

THE RISE OF MOBILE PHONES

In 2001, licences were granted to two mobile phone operators – the South African MTN and multinational Econet (now known as Vmobile), with the state-owned Nitel joining them in 2004. The introduction of mobile phones has been a blessing for millions who used to be frustrated by the inadequate land-line system.

Africa as a whole is the world's fastest-growing mobile phone market – increasing at a rate of 65 per cent a year – and nowhere more so than in Nigeria, where the use of mobile phones has now outstripped that of land-line phones. In Nigeria, the number of mobile phone subscribers has soared from 37,000 in 2000 to around 3.3 million in early 2004.

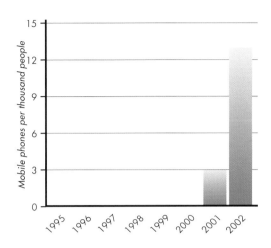

▲ Mobile phone use per 1,000 people, 1995-2002

Focus on: Email scams

Internet cafés in Lagos are being used by criminals to send scam emails all over the world. The criminals pose as people who need to get money out of Nigeria and ask for an advance fee to help them do this. Many people in the UK, the United States and elsewhere have fallen for these deceptions, and the Nigerian police are now locating and shutting down the Internet sites used by the scammers. In Nigeria, this type of crime is referred to as a '419', after the section of the Criminal Code of Nigeria that makes it illegal.

▼ A poster warns people about the hazards of Internet scams, known as 419s.

CHAPTER 10

Education and Health

Education is highly valued by most Nigerians but standards have fallen because of poverty and a lack of government investment. The government does not provide any free schooling, so parents have to pay for their children's education.

SCHOOLS AND UNIVERSITIES

Primary education for all was introduced in Nigeria in the 1970s and is compulsory for children between the ages of six and eleven. This policy is hard for the government to enforce, however, because parents cannot always afford to send their children to school. In all Nigerian communities, it is considered more important for boys to have an education in order to become the breadwinners, so girls are usually the first to be removed from school if money is short in their families. This is particularly true in Muslim areas, where less value is placed on girls having a formal education. This is reflected in the fact that literacy rates for women in the north are about 20 per cent lower than for women in the south.

Education and health data

- Life expectancy at birth, male: 46.3
- Life expectancy at birth, female: 47.3
- Infant mortality rate per 1,000: 99
- Under-five mortality rate per 1,000: 191.4
- Physicians per 1,000 people: 0.3
- Health expenditure as % of GDP: 1.4%
- Education expenditure as % of GDP: 0.9%
- Primary net enrolment: 37%
- Pupil-teacher ratio, primary: 41.1
- Adult literacy as % age 15+: 69.1

Sources: United Nations Agencies and World Bank

◀ For cultural reasons, more boys than girls get the benefit of education in Nigeria.

Children must pass the common entrance exam in order to go to secondary school. Only about 26 per cent of Nigeria's children attend secondary school. Students take the senior secondary school exam at the end of their last year, after which universities and colleges provide higher education. Nigeria has about 40 universities and 27 technical colleges, located in the main urban areas. However, many Nigerians prefer to go to the USA or the UK to study because qualifications from foreign universities are often prized more highly by employers.

EDUCATION SYSTEMS

European-style education was introduced to Nigeria by Christian missionaries in the 1840s. Children in the country's primary schools are usually taught in English and sometimes also in a local language. In Islamic communities, children attend religious schools called *madrassahs*, in which they learn sections of the Qur'an by heart and study Arabic. Students at these religious schools also learn about morals and respect, as well as subjects studied in the European-style schools.

In many rural areas, children are educated informally by working alongside their parents, by becoming apprentices, or by participating in community life. They learn a trade, such as farming

▲ This boy is studying in a *madrassah* near Kano, in northern Nigeria. *Madrassahs* offer an education based on Islamic teaching and are most widespread in the more Islamic north of the country.

or carpentry; and traditional crafts, such as leatherwork. They are also taught about their cultural traditions, survival skills and social activities. Children often receive this informal education alongside more formal Muslim and European-style schooling. But a few children only get informal education.

There is also a cultural tradition of 'fostering', by which parents send their child to live with a family in an urban centre, or abroad, so that the child can attend school. Families will often make great sacrifices in order to do this, in the

> **?** **Did you know?**
>
> Educated Nigerians often speak English, as well as one or two of Nigeria's 400 native languages, such as Yoruba, Hausa or Igbo.

hope that a better education will allow their child to get a well-paid job and help support the rest of the family.

POVERTY AND POOR HEALTH

Those Nigerians who can afford to pay for healthcare have access to very good, but expensive, private hospitals and clinics. However, for the majority, there is a shortage of medical facilities, supplies, equipment and staff, partly because many doctors and nurses decide to leave to find higher-paid work overseas.

The infant mortality rate in Nigeria is one of the highest in the world, at 99 per 1,000 live births in 2006. Common causes of infant mortality include diarrhoea, acute respiratory infections, measles and malaria, all of which are preventable. Nigeria has a relatively high rate of diabetes – estimated at 2 per cent of the population. The

▼ Life expectancy at birth, 1960-2002

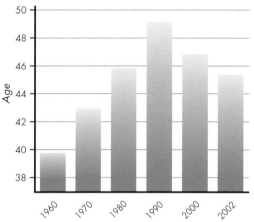

◀ Lack of basic services, especially lack of access to water, has a big impact on health. Many Nigerians have no running water and are forced to buy their water in plastic containers, like the ones being sold here.

incidence of sickle cell anaemia (a hereditary disease occurring mostly in those of African descent) is also high. Other common diseases are tuberculosis, malaria and polio.

There is often a direct connection between ill-health and poverty. The Nigerian government has set goals for improving the health service but it has a long way to go before meeting them. Total health expenditure in 2007 was 1.4 per cent of GDP. In the same year, the United States spent 15.4 per cent of GDP on health, and in the UK the figure was 8.1 per cent of GDP. According to the World Health Organization, Nigeria ranked near the bottom of the world's health systems –187th out of 190 countries – in 2000.

HIV/AIDS

Many cases of HIV/AIDS go unreported in Nigeria because of the stigma attached to the disease, but it is estimated that over 170,000 deaths in 2001 were attributable to AIDS. The stigma surrounding HIV/AIDS has made it difficult to educate people about the causes of the disease. There are few places where individuals can get tested for HIV/AIDS, and anti-retroviral drugs are too expensive for most. In 2007, there were more than a million AIDS orphans in Nigeria and nearly three million people thought to be infected with HIV.

> **Did you know?**
>
> In 2004, a new plant to manufacture anti-retroviral drugs opened in Lagos, set up and funded by Nigerian health professionals working in the United States. This centre aims to provide affordable treatment for those with HIV/AIDS.

◀ Federal government posters provide a way of warning people about the dangers of HIV/AIDS and telling them how to avoid infection.

Focus on: Polio immunization

In 2003, a polio immunization campaign was stopped in northern Nigeria because Islamic leaders in Kano began a (false) rumour that vaccines were contaminated with anti-fertility drugs as part of a US plot to stop Muslim women having children. As a result of the immunization programme stopping, the Global Polio Eradication Initiative traced new outbreaks of polio to the Kano area. Other African nations, including Mali and Guinea, that had been free of polio, also suffered polio outbreaks linked to those in Kano. In August 2004, polio vaccinations, with new supplies from Islamic countries in Asia, were restarted in northern Nigeria to bring the outbreak under control.

CHAPTER 11

Culture and Religion

In a country with so many different ethnic groups, some people think it is more accurate to talk of Nigeria's many different cultures rather than a single national culture. In reality, however, Nigeria's many ethnic groups share a lot of beliefs and practices.

The performing arts (especially plays, storytelling and dance) play an important role in Nigerian culture, for example. Such performances are often associated with cultural and religious holidays, and family events, such as weddings and naming ceremonies. All members of the extended family attend these functions, which usually include a lavish feast with as much food as the hosts can afford, and music to dance to. There is special music for different occasions, and these celebrations can go on for several days.

FAMILY LIFE

Extended families are the norm in Nigeria, particularly in rural areas. Parents, children, grandchildren and other relatives usually all live close to each other in a compound or under one roof. In urban areas, smaller, nuclear families are becoming more common but they still maintain strong links with their extended families and frequently visit or receive visitors. Nigerians have a strong sense of responsibility towards their families and their communities. In a country where there is no state support for the elderly, children and grandchildren have

always cared for their elderly relatives, but in some urban areas, particularly in the south, this practice is less common today.

Women in Muslim communities, especially those in northern Nigeria, are often kept in seclusion and are not permitted even to leave the home. They do all the domestic work, such as cooking, cleaning and caring for children. But in other parts of Nigeria, particularly in towns and cities, women are starting to lead more independent lives. They are usually the main traders and they are increasingly going out to work. Although many Muslim women's lives remain restricted, some are even getting involved in Nigerian politics. However, they often encounter opposition from some men and from some religious leaders.

► Life is changing for some Nigerian women. These Muslim women in Jigawa State are training to become tailors and run their own businesses.

FOOD

What Nigerians eat depends on how and where they live – whether urban or rural, in the north or the south – and what religion they follow. In the north, the diet is based on grains eaten with spicy vegetable sauces or a kind of kebab known as *tsire*. Muslims do not eat pork or drink alcohol. In the south, root crops such as yam and cassava are more often eaten, again with spicy, peppery stews and sauces. Fish is an important part of the Nigerian diet, except in the north, where goat is more commonly eaten. Fish is preserved by being smoked or dried. Snack foods, which can be bought from roadside stalls, include fried yam chips, meat pastries and doughnuts.

RELIGIOUS BELIEFS

The majority of Nigeria's Christians are found in the south, although a few live in the north. Most of the Yoruba people are Protestants and Anglicans, whereas the Igbo are mainly Catholic. Christianity was introduced to Nigeria by missionaries during the colonial period. In Yorubaland, in the south-west, evangelical/charismatic African churches have been founded, breaking away from the European-based form of Christianity. They have introduced African music and dance into their services.

▼ A large congregation crowds into an evangelical Pentacostalist Christian church in Lagos.

▲ Muslims at Friday prayers at a rural mosque in Kano State.

About half the people of Nigeria are Muslim. The Hausa and Fulani peoples in the north are predominantly Muslim, and a significant number of Yorubas are also Muslim. Daily prayers, attending a mosque, reading the Qur'an and following Islamic law are major elements of the Islamic faith. Every Muslim hopes to go on the *Hajj*, a pilgrimage to Mecca, in Saudi Arabia, at least once in his or her life.

During the month of Ramadan, which is the ninth month of the year in the Muslim calendar, Muslims fast during daylight hours. This is followed by the feast of *Eid-al-Fitr*. Traditional religions exist alongside Islam and Christianity. Followers of traditional religions often also pray to the Islamic god (Allah) and the Christian god, along with their own gods

? Did you know?

Nigeria began its film industry (known as Nollywood) in the 1970s. By 2004, it had become the third-largest in the world (after the Indian and United States film industries), producing over 2,000 low-budget films per year and distributing them on video all over Africa, where they are hugely popular.

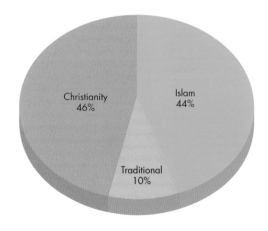

Christianity
46%

Islam
44%

Traditional
10%

▲ Major religions as percentage of total population

and ancestral spirits. Followers of traditional Nigerian religions believe in gods that live in natural elements such as rain and thunder. They also offer the spirits of their ancestors gifts, such as food, in return for help in their daily lives. For those who believe in ancestral spirits, a Nigerian funeral is an occasion for celebration because the person who has died is joining his or her ancestors.

▶ A traditional Nigerian religious practitioner (known as a juju man) in Benin City, with sacred pots and other objects that he uses to perform rituals.

 Did you know?

According to a survey conducted by the BBC in 2004, Nigeria is the most religious nation in the world. Over 90 per cent of Nigerians said they believed in a god, prayed regularly and would die for their religious beliefs.

Focus on: Masks and masquerades

A masquerade is an important ritual in many traditional religions in Nigeria, particularly among the Igbo people. According to Nigerian traditional religions, people are immortal and, through the use of masks and masquerades, dead ancestors can visit the land of the living. Most masquerades involve dancing and singing but they vary from one community to another. Costumes are made of grass, palm fronds, cloth or raffia, and masks are made from carved wood. Women, except those past childbearing age, are usually excluded from masquerades.

▶ A masquerade in Badagry, west of Lagos. The masquerade performers often dance in the street and ask their audience for money.

CHAPTER 12

Leisure and Tourism

The idea of organized leisure time is quite a new one in Nigeria. People in all communities have always found time to spend with family members and friends, talking about their lives or celebrating a birth, for example. But in the cities, in particular, life is changing fast and people are spending more time participating in activities and outings, such as visiting museums and parks and going to clubs and concerts.

LEISURE TIME IN RURAL AREAS

Nigerians in rural areas enjoy different leisure activities, especially festivals. Regattas are very popular on the rivers, for example, and there are festivals dedicated to crops and livestock, such as the Yam Festival in the south-east and the Crops Festival in Kaduna State.

NATIONAL HOLIDAYS

The religious festivals of the two main religions (Good Friday, Easter Monday, Christmas Day and Boxing Day for Christians, and Eid-al-Fitr, Eid-al-Kabir and Eid-al-Maulud for Muslims) are observed as national holidays by all Nigerians. People who have

▼ Young men enjoying themselves drumming, singing and dancing on the beach.

moved to the cities often return to their home villages for these occasions to spend them with other family members.

URBAN NIGHTLIFE AND MUSIC

In the cities, young people who can afford to do so flock to the cinemas and nightclubs. People dance all through the night and listen to a wide range of music styles, from Juju and Apala to Highlife (a fusion of western music and African music) and Makossa. Juju has a similar heavy beat to reggae. It started out as a style known as 'palm wine music', with banjos, guitars, shakers and hand drums. However, Juju groups today use more percussion instruments, as well as the electric guitar, and this type of music is now internationally famous. Popular stars of Juju music include King Sunny Ade and Chief Commander Ebenezer Obey.

▼ Boys play football in Kaduna, northern Nigeria.

GAMES

Across Nigeria, a game (known by the Yoruba as *ayo* and by the Hausa as *dara*) is played. Two people with a board and seeds or stones try to capture their opponents' seeds by landing in the same space. Young boys enjoy playing marbles, while girls are keener on skipping and clapping games involving rhythm and singing. Children often make their own toys out of recycled materials. For example, they may make a football from plastic bags and rubber bands and a spinning top from a coconut or a calabash.

? Did you know?

Famous Nigerian footballer Taribo West has an unusual background for a World Cup player. Having grown up as a juvenile street gang member in one of the toughest districts of Lagos, he now preaches as a Christian pastor when he isn't playing football.

SPORTS

Nigerians excel at sport of all kinds but football (or soccer) is by far the most popular in the country. In the 1996 Olympic Games, the Super Eagles, Nigeria's national football team, won the gold medal. Several Nigerian footballers, including Peter Odemwingie and Victor Ikpeba, moved to Europe, where they received high salaries. Nigerians have also excelled at an international level in track events and in boxing. Their team won the bronze medal in both the 4 x 100 metres and 4 x 400 metres relays at the 2004 Athens Olympics. The Nigerian boxer Mudeen Ganiyu made it to the quarter-finals in the Olympic Games in Athens in 2004. However, no Nigerian boxer has ever won an Olympic gold medal, even though the Nigerian government offered a prize of US$10,000 to any of its boxers who won a gold medal in 2004.

Among the Yoruba, traditional wrestling is very popular. There are several different kinds, such as *iga kadi*, which is like a free-for-all with very few rules, and *eke,* which has its own special techniques and rules. Traditional African games existed before colonists came to Nigeria and Nigerians are eager to preserve them.

TOURISM

Nigeria's turbulent past has prevented it from becoming a popular tourist destination. Potential visitors have been put off by periodic violence, high crime rates, poor infrastructure and the general disorganization of the country. However, with its vibrant culture and numerous artistic and natural attractions, Nigeria has great tourist potential. It has good

▼ Joan Elcah, a member of the Nigerian Olympic squad, in training before the 2004 Games in Athens.

beaches, such as those at Lekki near Lagos, dramatic scenery in the Eastern Highlands and around Jos, and a rich cultural mix of Arabic and European musical and architectural influences in places like Kano. It also has a thriving art and crafts scene and is well known for textiles and pottery. As a degree of stability has returned to Nigeria in recent years, the number of tourists has slowly increased. The Nigerian government is keen to develop the tourist industry further and sees it as one way of diversifying the country's economy and reducing its dependence on oil.

Tourism in Nigeria data

- Tourist arrivals, millions: 1.01
- Earnings from tourism in US$: 46,000,000
- Tourism as % foreign earnings: 0.1
- Tourist departures, millions: n/a
- Expenditure on tourism in US$: 1,385,000,000

Source: World Bank

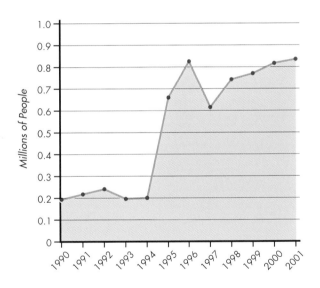

▲ Wikki Warm Springs, in Yankari National Park, central Nigeria, could be a potential tourist destination.

▲ Changes in international tourist arrivals, 1990-2001

Focus on: New opportunities for tourism

In 2004, the Nigerian tourist industry was very small but the government is targeting foreigners interested in the environment and African Americans interested in their heritage as possible tourists. Eco-tourism, such as bird-watching trips, and heritage tourism (trips to ancient sites), offer exciting opportunities for Nigeria's future tourism industry. The old slave-trading town of Badagry, with its Museum of Slave Trade and early missionaries' cemeteries, is being developed as a tourist attraction. The ancient walled cities in the north, with their Islamic architecture and colourful markets, could also attract visitors in the future.

CHAPTER 13

Environment and Conservation

Nigeria's natural environment is under considerable stress from expanding population, poverty and the effects of people's actions, such as cutting down trees. Because of all these problems, the environment may eventually become incapable of supporting Nigeria's growing population and poverty will increase.

DEFORESTATION AND LAND DEGRADATION

For hundreds of years, people have been cutting down Nigeria's trees to clear space for agricultural land or to obtain building materials and fuel. Nigeria originally had forest cover of around 72,000 sq km (27,800 sq miles). By 2004, this was down to 10,000 sq km (3,860 sq miles), and the country's forests are still being cleared at the rate of around 14 per cent a year. Recent depletion is the result of road building and clearing of land for farms and pasture, as well as logging (much of which is illegal).

The lack of vegetation, the removal of trees that hold the soil in place, and heavy rainfall have led to particularly bad soil erosion, especially on the Jos Plateau, where there is a high density of population and poor soil. In the north, deforestation, irrigation and over-grazing are leading to land degradation and desertification (the process by which land becomes barren and starts to resemble a desert). These processes threaten to destroy rare plant and animal species and render the land useless for farming.

▼ Soil erosion, here in the Jos Plateau region, is caused by the removal of vegetation.

Environmental and conservation data

🗁 Forested area as % total land area: 2

🗁 Protected area as % total land area: 6

🗁 Number of protected areas: 1,009

SPECIES DIVERSITY

Category	Known species (1992-2002)	Threatened species
Mammals	274	27
Breeding birds	286	9
Reptiles	154	2
Amphibians	53	n/a
Fish	95	2
Plants	4,715	119

Source: World Resources Institute

URBAN POLLUTION

Many Nigerian cities suffer from polluted water supplies, bad sanitation and inadequate sewage systems. In addition, heavy traffic and poorly maintained vehicles produce considerable air pollution. Pollutants that contaminate air, water and soil resources are also generated by industries that are often poorly regulated. In Kano, for example, pollution from abattoirs, tanneries and factories seriously threatens the quantity and quality of local water resources. Furthermore, this region's low and unreliable rainfall means that toxic elements that accumulate in the water systems are not flushed away regularly by the flow of water. Instead the toxins become concentrated, and contaminate the water sources. But the government is now trying to intervene to reduce pollution. For instance, it has banned the importing of vehicles over five years old so as to cut the number of old, polluting vehicles on Nigeria's roads.

▶ In the absence of a waste collection service, people are forced to dump their rubbish alongside city streets, such as here on the outskirts of Kano.

▲ A child goes home to a shack on Bonny Island in the Niger Delta. Many people in this part of Nigeria live in similarly harsh conditions.

Focus on: Oil pollution in the Niger Delta

The exploitation of oil has had a devastating effect on the Niger Delta. The land has been subjected to oil spills, and the groundwater has been polluted. Much of the pollution is a result of local people breaking into oil pipelines to steal oil to sell on the black market. In 2004, the Nigerian government reported that thefts from oil pipelines amounted to 500,000 barrels per day (worth around US$12 billion a year). Oil pollution has badly affected the Delta region's fragile forests and mangrove swamps and has had a disastrous impact on the people there, many of whom make their living from farming and fishing.

WILDLIFE

In the early twentieth century, Nigeria was still home to elephants, buffaloes, lions and leopards. Many of these animals have now disappeared because people hunted them for their meat. In addition, their habitats have been destroyed by urbanization, deforestation, land clearance, road building and other human activities. Nigeria's endangered species are found only in major reserves, zoos or very remote areas. Much of Nigeria's other wildlife is seriously threatened. Around 10 per cent of mammal species and 3 per cent of bird species, for example, are threatened with extinction.

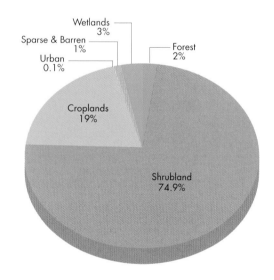

▲ Habitat type as percentage of total area

WHAT IS BEING DONE?

Among Nigeria's over 1,000 protected areas are twelve game and forest reserves and eight national parks, where wildlife is protected. The Omo Forest Reserve, 135 km (84 miles) north-east of Lagos, has African forest elephants, chimpanzees and other endangered species. Here, researchers and environmentalists carry out scientific studies of the wildlife and try to prevent poaching and illegal logging. Many traditional farming practices, that have been used for centuries and are still being used, such as planting trees and hedgerows, terracing steep slopes and applying manure, are now being recognized as sustainable ways of farming, conserving and managing the land.

Nigeria's Federal Environmental Protection Agency was established in 1988 but has so far had little impact. However, the high court's ruling in 2006 that gas flaring is illegal will in time not only reduce greenhouse gas emissions, but will also provide both more gas for domestic consumption and more gas for export via the West Africa Gas Pipeline. Nigeria also co-operates with its neighbours, Cameroon, Chad and Niger, in the joint management of wildlife in the Chad Basin. Many conservation groups, such as the World Wide Fund for Nature, are campaigning to try to ensure that the government protects the environment and to force the oil companies to prevent oil leaks.

▼ Giraffes roam in Yankari National Park.

Focus on: Nigeria's rainforest

Around 95 per cent of Nigeria's original tropical rainforest, most of it in Cross River State, has been destroyed. However, the Nigerian government has now made logging illegal in this area. This is a critical step in protecting one of West Africa's last remaining tropical forests. Cross River's forests still contain gorillas, chimpanzees, forest elephants, and the highly endangered drill monkey. These forests also protect the watershed on which more than 300 rural communities depend.

Focus on: Grey parrots

Conservationists are increasingly concerned about the growing trade in grey parrots. According to the Convention on International Trade in Endangered Species (CITES), only limited trade is allowed under strict licensing. However, it is estimated that each year between 5,000 and 10,000 grey parrots are smuggled from forests in eastern Nigeria and then sold in Asia and the Middle East. These parrots are very popular because they are able to mimic human speech.

CHAPTER 14

Future Challenges

Since about 2006, a dramatic increase in oil prices has seen Nigeria's economy grow very rapidly and the World Bank now ranks Nigeria as one of the world's top fifty wealthiest economies. Despite this, there remain close to 70 per cent of Nigerians who struggle to live on less than US$1 per day.

POVERTY

There is an enormous gap between the rich and the poor in Nigeria. According to a 2004 World Bank report, about 80 per cent of Nigeria's oil and natural gas revenues goes to just 1 per cent of the country's population. This combination of poverty for the vast majority, and wealth for a small minority, means that people feel desperate and resentful, and it has often led to unrest in the country. With a stable, civilian government, more answerable to the people, Nigerians hope that the potential wealth, energy and talent that exist in Nigeria could lead to a country that is self-reliant and prosperous, where revenues from natural resources are invested more equally and sustainably.

▼ Barefoot kids beg for money outside a supermarket and Internet café used by richer Nigerians. There is great inequality in many of Nigeria's urban centres.

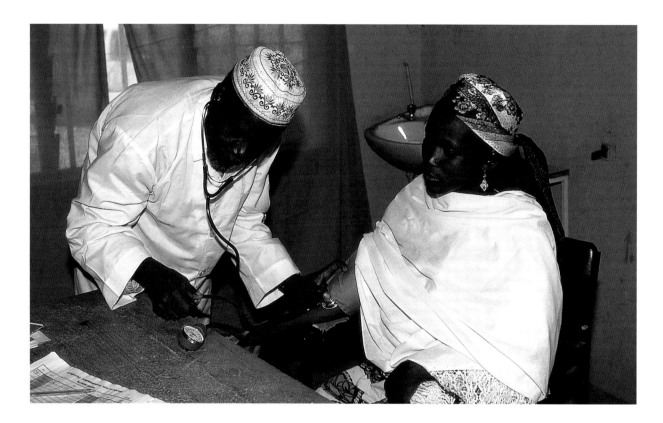

▲ Local health clinics, like this one near Kano, play a crucial role in the fight against HIV/AIDS.

HIV/AIDS

Whatever progress Nigeria's government is able to make in developing its economy and stabilizing its society will be undermined if it is not able to stem the increase in HIV/AIDS infection. The National Intelligence Council in the United States has identified Nigeria as one of the five countries that is facing a drastic increase in HIV/AIDS, and this crisis puts severe strain on its government's resources.

Nigeria has been slow to confront the HIV/AIDS epidemic. But the government is now taking action – training health workers, providing preventive counselling and expanding AIDS testing facilities – in 2005 there was a slight decline in the number of people becoming infected with HIV, and

US$862 million of national and international money was spent in 2006 to tackle this problem.

NATIONAL UNITY

Any government of Nigeria has the challenge of reconciling the demands of the diverse ethnic and religious groups within the country. Major tensions continue to exist over access to resources. This has led some people to wonder whether Nigeria should remain as one country, as originally created by British colonizers, or break apart into several separate states. The experience of the Biafra War is still vivid in the minds of many Nigerians and affects their thinking. A survey in 2001 found that most Nigerians wanted the nation to remain intact. Only one person in five thought the differences between Nigerians were too strong to overcome, and that the country should be divided.

Timeline

9000 BC Earliest evidence of human habitation in Nigeria.

500 BC–AD 200 Nok Culture flourishes.

AD 900 Emergence of kingdom of Kanem around Lake Chad, and establishment of Igbo civilization.

1100 Establishment of Yoruba city-states.

Late 1400 Arrival of Portuguese traders.

1500 Peak of the Benin kingdom.

1804 Muslim holy wars (jihads) against the Hausa and Yoruba city-states.

1807 Britain outlaws the slave trade.

1861 Lagos is annexed by the British.

1884 Berlin Conference in which Africa is divided up between European powers.

1886 The Yoruba wars.

1990 Declaration of Nigeria as two protectorates.

1914 Unification of Nigeria into one state.

1950s Discovery of oil in Nigeria.

1960 Nigeria gains its independence from Britain.

1963 Nigeria becomes a federal republic.

1966 Nigeria becomes a military regime.

1967-1970 Biafra War.

1971 Nigeria joins OPEC.

1976 Nigerian capital is moved from Lagos to Abuja.

1979-83 A brief period of civilian rule in Nigeria.

1986 Wole Soyinka wins Nobel Prize for Literature.

1991 Ben Okri wins UK Booker Prize for his novel, *The Famished Road*.

1991 Census held in Nigeria.

1996 Nigeria's soccer team wins the Olympic gold medal.

1999 Nigeria returns to civilian democratic rule.

2000 Declaration of Sharia law (Islamic law) in several northern Nigerian states.

2002 Establishment of the African Union.

2003 Nigeria launches its own satellite from Russia.

Glossary

Annex (Of a country or state) to take control of.

Anti-retroviral drugs Medicines used to treat the HIV/AIDS virus.

Apartheid A system of government introduced in South Africa in 1948 to keep black, white, mixed-race and Asian people separate and unequal.

Autonomous rule Self-government by a state or group of people.

Biodiversity Variety of forms of life.

Calabash A large, hard fruit with a shell that can be dried and used as a bowl.

City-state A city which, with the surrounding country area, forms an independent state.

Civilian government A non-military, democratic government, made up of elected representatives.

Coup An event that occurs when a group of people suddenly get together to try to overthrow those in power.

Delta An area of low, fertile land where a river divides into branches towards the sea.

Diabetes A disease in which there is too much sugar in the blood.

Economic Community of West African States (ECOWAS) A regional group of sixteen West African countries, founded in 1975.

Eco-tourism Tourism that is sensitive to its impact on environments and local people.

Equatorial (Of climate) near the equator; very hot.

Evangelical/charismatic churches Certain fundamentalist Protestant Christian churches which place particular emphasis on the importance of faith, studying the Bible and public preaching.

Federal capital The capital of the whole country, as opposed to the capital of a state within the country.

Global warming The gradual warming of the Earth's atmosphere as a result of carbon dioxide emissions and other greenhouse gases trapping heat.

Gross Domestic Product (GDP) The total market value of all goods and services produced in a country.

HIV/AIDS Human Immunodeficiency Virus (HIV) is a virus spread by unprotected sex or contaminated needles or blood supplies. It can develop into Acquired Immuno-Deficiency Syndrome (AIDS), which is fatal.

Human rights The non-political rights of freedom, equality, etc, which belong to any person without regard to race, religion, colour or sex.

Independence (Of a country) the right to control its own affairs.

Infant mortality The number of babies, out of every 1,000 born, who die before the age of one.

Infrastructure Networks that allow communication and/or help people and the economy to function, e.g. roads, railways, electricity and phone lines.

Malaria A tropical disease transmitted to people by mosquito bites.

Mangrove A semi-submerged tropical forest found in coastal regions of the tropics.

Palm-oil Oil obtained from the nut of an African palm tree; used widely in West African cooking.

Protectorate A country controlled and protected by a more powerful nation that takes charge, especially of its defence and foreign affairs.

Sedimentary Made from bits of rock and soil that have been gathered, moved around and then left in a place by water or ice.

Semi-arid Receiving less than 100-600 mm (4-24 inches) rain per year.

Tuberculosis An infectious disease that attacks many parts of the body, especially the lungs.

Watershed The dividing line separating two river basins.

Further Information

BOOKS TO READ

The Changing Face of Nigeria
Rob Bowden and Roy Maconachie
(Hodder, 2003)

Economically Developing Countries: Nigeria
Alasdair Tenquist
(Hodder, 1995)

Agricultural Change in Nigeria
Kathleen Baker
(Murray, 1989)

Countries of the World: Nigeria
Achu Kamala and James Morris
(Hodder Wayland, 1992)

The Wealth of Nations: Nigeria
J. Ayliffe
(Hodder Wayland, 1998)

NOVELS

Things Fall Apart
Chinua Achebe
(Heinemann, 1983)

The Famished Road
Ben Okri
(Vintage, 1992)

The Slave Girl
Buchi Emecheta
(George Braziller, 1980)

Purple Hibiscus
Chimamanda Ngozi Adichie
(Fourth Estate, 2004)

USEFUL WEBSITES

www.motherlandnigeria.com/geography.html
Basic information about Nigeria.

www.nigeriatoday.com
A portal site to all Nigeria's newspapers, which can be read online free of charge.

www.allafrica.com/nigeria
News articles about Nigeria.

Index

Page numbers in **bold** indicate pictures.

About the Authors

Ali Brownlie Bojang, worked as a teacher for ten years, before becoming an education officer for Oxfam. She is the author of several books on Africa, including *We Come From Nigeria* and *We Come From South Africa*.

Rob Bowden is a freelance author and photographer who specializes in Africa and African issues. He has taught at several UK universities and written numerous children's books about Africa.